The Afflicted Moments

Volume 1

By: Mr. Maurice Campbell

The Afflicted Moments Volume 1
Maurice Campbell ©2018

For events, questions or comments please contact
 Campbell Promotions and Marketing
(770)609-7384
Email: 1mrmauricecampbell@gmail.com

Table of contents

- **Bit too much**
- **A new family**
- **His tolerance became short**
- **Feeling better to do better**
- **So much for loyalty**
- **His only regret**
- **Before she left**
- **The question of marriage**
- **Dreams! Dreams! Dreams!**
- **Loving the company**
- **Help all around**
- **Thinking alike**
- **Still sticking around**
- **When he turned**
- **He just can't shake the thought of her**
- **The visitor**
- **Looking in the wrong direction**
- **Pure love**
- **He just can't settle *reduce font size bring over to right**
- **What is substance?**
- **Treating others**

- Learning!
- You are there
- Reality hits hard again
- To have or not to have
- Another day Another defeat
- Yes and maybe yes
- Not made to be handled
- It's the way
- Waking up every morning
- Just hanging out
- Changing everything
- Just the other day
- Keep talking please
- His worrying
- What does it mean?
- Made up mind
- A fulfilling prayer
- Clever, Smart, Witty, and whatever
- A point
- Back in church
- Breaking up

- Fake love or real love
- Why stopping
- Swap!
- The way
- Grown woman
- This have to be love
- GROWN MAN
- Kicking up the rocks
- Forgiveness
- Why am I here
- Confused
- Body, Soul, and Mind
- YOU!
- A Good break indeed
- He See
- Caught up in a fantasy
- Afraid!!!!
- Torture
- The definition of feelings
- Ruining
- Loving

- **The road**
- **Him meeting her**
- **Living this new life**
- **Mistreated only for a while**
- **A Renewed Love**
- **Away He went**
- **Highly favored**
- **Calling All unbelievers**
- **Getting Weary**
- **Given the words**
- **God give Him strength**
- **How many times**
- **Free but yet still bound**
- **Facial Expressions**
- **Finally Revealed**
- **Forgiveness Does come**
- **He caught a glimpse**
- **Led by God or by man**
- **Mad as Hell * BRING TITLE TO MIDDLE**
- **MISSED ONE**
- **My House**

- No one to call
- Pleasant
- Revived
- The Call
- There when Needed
- This is the time
- When everything else has failed
- Fight
- If he told you
- Remembering the time
- Accident on standby
- Words
- Waiting to Unveil
- Punk out spirit
- Through it all
- Thanking God
- If you were happy for him
- Thank you Lord
- His Handy Helper
- The perfect Christmas gift
- Beauty Defined

- **Overwhelmed On Every Side**
- **If I AM…**
- **Only One**
- **The way she Thinks**
- **If she was a bird**
- **Just who she is…**
- **The Works**
- **Where could they be?**
- **To Be or Not to Be a Fool**
- **He had to swear**
- **Just Wanting to**
- **He lack No More**
- **His Goodness and Mercy**
- **Missing Her The Most**
- **God Showed Him**
- **Two broken hearts Equals One**
- **It was all too easy**
- **Letting Go Everyday**
- **The King in search of a Queen**
- **Containing the Love**
- **Added Light**

Introduction

I started writing The Afflicted Moments Volume 1 by no accident because of my plight for the truth, and my fight for the truth that is still being fought everyday which means there is a lot more than we see going on that someone else needs to know that is seeking the truth. Then it's passed the time that I release what a lot of people are dying or have died in secret wanting to know if anyone else out there is going through what they are constantly going through? Therefore how can I myself learn from these moments and make it past the point of no return to what I'm going thru? How can others learn of themselves in the same aspect? In reading this book revelations will be made, notes will be taken. So if you require reading glasses put them on for you want miss a word and if you are eating while you read try not to drop nothing on your book that might be the poem that brings about a sure deliverance. Knowing that God has already made us free! We put ourselves back into bondage and captivity!!

About the author

Maurice Campbell a very talented individual born on May 29, 1985 to Ms. Barbara Campbell and Mr. Johnny Owens at Houston Healthcare Complex in Warner Robins, Georgia. A young man who believes in seeking God first in all things but yet easily admits he hasn't arrived God is not done with him yet. Obtained a Diploma in Mindfulness and have various certificates of completion. The author of "103 Simple and Practical Relationship Tips and Thoughts". . Furthermore he tell others that being a full time writer and author allows him to exercise the gifts God has placed inside of him and to reach beyond the walls and gates society has installed in our minds.

Dedications

This book is dedicated to all those near and far who has encouraged me through the years and has even went out their way to lend me a helping hand in various times of my life. I just can't thank everyone enough! Much Love …..

AFFLICTED

Thank you Lord for afflicting him building and tearing things up and flipping some upside down so he may give you all the glory in these times because it's your will not his even though he don't always see it that way so it don't matter how many times he write his plans on paper or on his blackberry it will not make a difference especially if it is not what you have plan so continue full speed ahead

Afflict!

Afflict!!

Afflict!!!

He Stays

He stays up all night thinking about all the fun times they shared walking around stores in the twelve o'clock hour or later. Both bored with nothing to do. Tickling and poking each other at any given moment. They didn't even want to stay home and just watch TV. however it didn't use to be like that when they first met they were kind of distant he was just liking the way she walk but as they were discussing the times that passed by and all the years they have actually known each other he also endured some tough times and when the those tough times were over there weren't too many around left he could call friend and there she was they picked up right where they left off as friends if those tough times he had endured never happened still liking the way she walk and more! Then one day out of nowhere he started to develop feelings for her. In his mind anything he could do for her he would do it times three. The words she spoke in that year was like keys unlocking a door that has been sealed shut by a team of welders and all it took was her that's right one person to make him feel like the way he now does, and he ended up talking, thinking, and staying up all night worrying about her praying that one day it would get better than this between them. Its sounds crazy to him even though he has to follow what he think is his heart. As he says the most "I want somebody to like me for me not what I can give to them" and now he truly believes he found just that he wouldn't want her to change nothing that's right not a thing but he would allow without any hesitations the God he serve change her or the whole situation.

<u>He really didn't want her to leave</u>

The day came that he really didn't expect to come or happened. Especially the way it did, when the words came out of her mouth "I am leaving" after he heard that he really felt like he lost the most precious treasure he have ever had in his entire life. After all the painstaking, heartbreaking, and patience spent looking for the one that clearly defined in his dictionary as a help mate because that all she did when they were around each other he couldn't help himself or prevent himself from hiding his feelings for that particular person. But yet he still hid them feeling deep down inside that it still isn't the right time. Asking him when will be the right time. Those words alone that he never spoke struck something in his heart which had him thinking of ways he could keep her here close by to him. He even prayed she stays down here only because he had fear of never finding anyone like her again. Trying his best to hang on to the times they shared and not beat himself up when the day comes that he can no longer ride down the street and wait patiently for the girl he thought he had fell in love with to come outside. The best thing about their relationship he always thought she knew how he felt about her through all the jokes and conversations they had. So he prays as life goes on waiting on that day the lord bless him with the things he need which will also be the day he be able to keep her closer and closer and closer…….. And if she does end up leaving someone with her qualities and more will take her place.

On To the Better Days

Times have changed frowns became a part of my nature but that was then. A new day has arrived I am speeding off into the better days ahead not looking back but forward to the better days ahead knowing if I wait upon the lord he shall renew my strength, replacing all that was lost even me, lost was I, but off to my better days. Nothing now but smiles and laughter and greater moments I have every day seeking his face, his promises. Laughing myself to sleep in the joy in the lord!!!!!!

Dead Flies

Dead flies!

Dead flies!

Where are the dead flies?

Why I don't see any around me even though them around a lot

Of people but not me?

Dead flies, Dead flies where are the dead flies?

I am glad I can't see them or have them around me!!!

DEAD FLIES!!

DEAD FLIES!!

Ecclesiastes 10:1 King James Version- Dead flies cause the ointment of the apothecary to send fourth a stinking savour: so doth a little folly him that is in reputation for wisdom and honour

Ecclesiastes 10:1 New International Version

As dead flies give perfume a bad smell, so a little folly outweighs wisdom and honor

Shaking the association he didn't need

Yeah he hung out with the ones who cursed like a drunken sailor. The ones who defile every woman that cross their paths and the woman who defiled every man that cross their path in their mind he felt the only reason why to hang out or to keep his association with them varied on the things he got accomplished with them. They acted to him more like friends then his own. Even though they never step one foot in a church if he wanted something done the saints will not get a call they will. They always get it done. Which might be the point Satan has them connected just to keep unclean spirits around him. Instead of him being free from all he is bound by some.

What he spoke to the lord in his days of misery

"Show me what to do to stay away from things not in your

kingdom.

I know I have a lot of void time on my hands. It's seemed to be

getting harder every day. I wonder away from home and from you

lord and at the end of each day I always wonder my way back

home. Show, tell, or whatever method you want to use. Occupy my

time so that it may benefit the kingdom. I want to be free from

familiar spirits. I am tired of failing and feeling drained by my

surroundings.

What else can I do for this not to happen?

What mighty word must I hear?"

Now since he heard her voice

Now since he heard her voice he feels comfortable that she is out of harm's way. Thanking the lord for watching out for her as she goes out of her zone to be there for a love one.

Now since he heard her voice he slips into a reflection moment thinking about what place they would be today if she was where he is and ends up talking about her nonstop to his best family members who *sometimes* provide positive feedback. Thinking that was the time he actually realized he might actually really cares for her a whole lot.

Oh No! this is not just a care for the physical aspect of her but her mind, body, and soul furthermore he for one will not be giving up on her

NOW SINCE HE HEARD HER VOICE………. If he could and if he had control over the world turning it would stop when he is with her………..

No one listened to him

Times flew by but no one in the house listens to him. Majority of the times what he say its correct or it be for their benefit but they ignore him time after time making him angry and angrier at the situation leaving him to figure out or try to figure out why are they ears stop up when several stores sells Q-tips some even stay open twenty four hours a day what excuse could they possible use to not take heed to his words of warnings and his words of wisdom. So now he does no more talking but a whole lot of walking, and there will be no more reacting but a lot of acting.

No Need For Him To Cry

There was no need for him to cry over her or anybody else he knew that the lord will continue to watch over her and guide her thoughts and one day she will realize he has always been there.

There was no need for him to cry because the God he serves is all powerful and all-knowing so no matter what comes his way he is the one waiting to fight. He is a person that don't like to be defeated but victorious in all the things he place his hands on in all areas Christ leads him to walk on!
In all things Christ leads him to speak on!

There was no need for him to cry he knew where all his help come from as family did nothing in helping him reach his true calling in Christ but the Crown goes out to him that fought the good fight and continue to fight. The crown of the righteous…. There was no need…There was no need...but there was a need a need for him to pray. That's right pray!

Bit too much

He bit too much in a race he was running by himself he bit too much. Racing to be the first when he already was the first with the tools God has already place in his possession. Thinking if he bit off the right amount surely riches will follow. But as he leans into his own understanding instead of the understanding of the Lord things gets worse and that bite he took was making him feel stressed out, overwhelmed and frustrated everyday he had to face what he bit off. Wondering to himself that if he could ignore them for a couple of days or until the end of that month he might be okay because that month was so full of events good and bad ones that he wanted to just ride away from it all but God stepped in and smooth things out. And for him I am able to sing.......

"What A Mighty God We serve"

" What A Mighty God We Serve "…..

A New Family

A new family he met indeed but an old family at the same time. The way they met shouldn't never took place at that moment of mourning a love one, but to him if that's how he could meet his new family then so be it, that day he also met his brother he heard lots of talk about. But he mention to a lot that knowing where he come from might be the key to why he felt so lost like there was something else he need to know his knowledge of his heritage was missing in his mind. He sought after that because he wanted to know why things in his life just kept happening all the time. As he met them he felt more relieved because by him knowing that more family existed and yet did nothing to get to know them weigh on him harder than him not knowing. Which was the only way things got better to him having now the opportunity to offer the new family what he has inside of him.......... CHRIST

His Tolerance became short

His tolerance became short. Whatever gave him the idea he could put up with it he never quite figure it out. Trying his very best not to lose his cool he would walk out the house and camp outside. They never knew where he goes. In fact they never asked either. They just knew he wasn't in the house no more. He came to one conclusion family support may never come his way, but what made him happy is when he speaks to himself asking these questions "Who is my mother? Who is my father? Who is my brother? Who is my sister?" and the answers from those questions came from within ....The Word of God

Matthew 12:48 King James Bible- But he answered and said unto him that told him, Who is my mother? And who are my brethren

Feeling Better To Do Better

Feeling better to do better! Therefore no sickness doesn't exist in his mind how about yours? In order for sickness to exist it might be time for an exam by the firstborn among many brothers. So something is wrong because it's impossible to have Christ dwelling on the inside of us and sickness at the same time without any combat going on. When will the fighting begin? Don't know for yourself so how should anyone else know? After all it is your fight!!!

Romans 8:29 King James version – For whom he did foreknow, he also did predestinate to be conformed to the image of his Son, that he might be the firstborn among many brethren.8

*Romans 8:9 King James Version- But ye are not in the flesh, but in the spirit, if so be that the Spirit of God Dwell in you. If anyone does not have the Spirit of Christ, he does not belong to him**

So much for loyalty

So much for loyalty as he wakes up thinking to himself getting ready for a great day or at least that's what he thought thinking that everything will be brought back the way he left it off but everyone he spoke with in all areas of his life had changed on him. He summarized it in his mind the only answer is that God has another plan in store for him so he didn't give up he stop doing what most was telling him to do because he tried all he could try and the results looked pretty ugly but it didn't stop him just made him more focused.

Jeremiah 29:11 King James Version- For I know the thoughts that I think toward you, said the LORD, thoughts of peace, and not of evil, to give you an expected end.

His only regret

His only regret was not having the necessary funding to establish himself better than before and to be able to help a particular person in a way they have never been helped before knowing that that particular person deserve to have a chance at obtaining the best and nothing less. He never knows why he has such strong feelings for that particular person they kind of snuck up on him. Leaving him thinking that may be her assignment from God to him and that that entire particular person was supposed to do is allow him to care for someone like never before. Trying to figure that out he continues to pray but adds this to it "Dear Lord please don't let this one end up on the disappointment list but if it is your will let your will be done ..."

Before She Left

Before she left town the words he wanted to say was "I wanted to let you know you brought in more light to my life. To me you were my only best friend that I can chill with without watching the time because when I was with you time didn't matter. I don't think I can find no one to take the place you took in my life the memories we have together will live on forever. You made me feel like I have nothing at all to worry about. The only worries you brought to me is the worrying I do when you have gone far away praying that God shields you. You are just not somebody to me that can be easily forgotten which is tearing me up into pieces on the inside because I don't want you to go but stay here with me and hangout I know its selfish of me to be that way but I can't help it trying to swallow that you are actually leaving is like pouring drain'O down the pipes and it want go down to break up the blockage but sits on top of it but if you must go you have my support." I can't help but to wonder will he ever have the courage to tell her?

The question of marriage

The question of marriage always stayed on his mind but his focus no! What he always wanted was nothing more than family of his own some one that is affectionate, caring, loving and much more. Every day he sees potential in one of his friends. She knows that she has the potential so he always wondering what will it take to unlock that potential for her to be the woman in his life he always dream of the once in a lifetime Godly marriage that requires no need to be repeated, every night of this current year he been thinking about her a lot. The truth of it all he wants so desperately to tell her but he feels that it isn't the right time due to their lives at this present time.

Dreams! Dreams! Dreams!

What do they mean?

Who can he tell?

Who can he not tell?

Dreams comes and goes to him and to his brothers and sisters in the bible, but when they had a dream it was a message from God instructing them to do something or a warning about an event soon to happen.

Dreams good ones, bad ones, crazy ones, weird ones we still have them no way out of that scientific fact! But it's the weird ones he didn't quite understand maybe because of what the dream consists of that it was either hard to believe or impossible in his mind but yet reminding himself whatever God releases in heaven he will release it on earth to do his will! This guidance he constantly wanted in his life. He went to sleep every night knowing and thinking God can and will speak to him in his sleep giving clarity to things on the mind. When just that happened he would

awake the next morning thinking about just that one dream

thinking when do whatever happened in his dream actually

happen in real life when he is

WIDE AWAKE.......

Loving the company

Loving the company with no bad times while they are around each other, in fact if he had an option of doing that every day he would do just that. Beating him in the smile contest, and beating him in the caring jokes category without knowing offering him a way of escape by being the person she is made him feel more relaxed than any wine he rarely had tasted. A couple more pleasant experiences like that he just might pop that BIG question on her he just waiting patiently and making things better in his life as the sun comes up and down followed by the moon in like manner.

Help all around

As his struggle in his life he sometimes wonders who is around him to help in this situation. Ignoring the help he had all along all he had to do is pick up the phone and get back on board success never came to anyone who didn't deserve it like he did knowing for himself success can be achieved no matter how many times it seem like it wasn't going to work in his favor it does. So of course by now he is more energetic than ever ready to learn the right way from his mentors that notified him to stick close to them he can't fail…….. As Paul of Taraus written in *1 Corinthians 11:1 Be ye followers of me, even as I also am of Christ*

<u>Thinking Alike</u>

Both sit there and laugh and sometime ends up saying the same exact thing then pause for a minute then resume laughing again because they know each other to well facing similar challenges wondering for themselves how are they going to make it out and overcome their struggle and just maybe when their storms in life is reduced maybe they can take some big steps together in life and do their thing. Whatever their thing happens to be I am sure they will be happy doing just that as they continue to ignore the ones they need to.......

Still sticking around

There she goes still sticking around not knowing that he never intended for her to leave as those days supposedly draw near those same exact days draw further and further away and he isn't mad at all. In fact how much he dislikes delays he ends up loving this delay and maybe he will get that opportunity to blow her mind away. In a shocking sense because how can one know so much already and continue to carry on the same way showing no difference. So now here is a good point for him to ask her first "how she really feels about him?" Praying that those past hurt emotions and relationships don't turn theirs sour and that she will be able to trust him with anything from A to Z.

When He Turned

When he turned around his words that were thought of first was "she has truly added more light to my paths I can walk in darkness all day and see through the darkness with the light she has brought unto me" as his eyes laid upon a site of beauty he can never recall seeing until that day, it was an awesome site. One that will keep a glowing smile upon his face despite what anyone else may think. One you will find digging up lost artifacts in Egypt a lasting memory indeed that will have a home in his memory no matter what happens it will last forever!

He Just Can't Shake The thought of her

There he goes up all night thinking about a girl, not just any ole girl. She was locked in to his heart. Tired? Never around her as a matter of fact had he actually become more energetic when they together wanted so badly to give her the world she meant that much to him so you can bet your dollars nobody dared to talk about her in a bad way why he is around. Not losing a bit of sleep because when it was that time for him to sleep he just close his eyes and think about her for those few seconds.

The Visitor

The visitor came by surprise but yet he still took her in like he was expecting that all along. Three whole days he put aside his agenda and help the visitor tend to theirs. Three whole days he didn't even count the money he spent helping the visitor get to where she was trying to go. Three whole days he gave up his room and slept in the living room not mad at all. He just knew all she cried is HELP! The only right thing to do was what he did without asking permission from no human form but from God alone. Not one negative lustful thought crossed his mind as he peeks into the room they were sleeping in he was just overwhelmed with joy that he could help them and teach them ways to remain strong in the midst of their storm as he then take the drive for the first time to drop the visitor off he soon thought she would be back but the reason why still remains a mystery……………..

Looking in the wrong direction

Yes times were great between the two of them but yet they were from two different worlds he was all about business and he always felt like she didn't even know what she was about. It took to many years for him to actually realize that only because he wanted her to be the girl in his life in the wrong way. She was cute with not too many brain cells to be working properly. He thinking to himself there got to be something wrong why hasn't she just cave in to his sweet tempting words he spoke to her every day. So much that it soon became clear to him he was wasting the breath God breathe into him that day because it was never worth it. Looking in that direction for years will take some time for him to look in another direction.

<u>Pure love</u>

Intro:

What are you looking for dirty love? No dirty love here only pure love, yep that's right pure love. A love that doesn't fade away like a fine mist spray but one that sticks to you like fresh wax on a freshly stripped floor. A love that says

"I love you by listening to all your problems good and bad

I love you by not telling you but by just being there without inserting self needs into the equation.

The word alone couldn't compete against the action took due to the love that is being put out

Love is not misunderstood but overlooked because of the eyes that are blinded by other forces

Love, Love, Love is all but with all that love there is...............

NO Greater Love"

LOVE HAS ME OPEN

AS PURE AS IT IS

SHE FEELS WHAT SHE FEELS

YES IT'S REAL

SIMPLE AND PLAIN HE CANT HELP BUT TO REMEMBER

HER NAME

AS IT RUNS THROUGH HIS MIND REPEATEDLY

AFRAID BECAUSE HE DOES NOT KNOW IF IT WILL LAST

BESIDES WHAT LAST LONGS ANYWAY?

PURE LOVE DOES...

Love me-

The word LOVE is an action verb.

He Just Can't Settle

He just can't settle for the life he now lives knowing that it is the
only temporary

He push himself morning until the next day trying to make it

better *never mind* he might experience some sickness or his feet

may hurt from

Wearing incorrect shoes it must be done in his mind hurting or

Not so that one day he will understand what his father meant

When he said "All is well"

What is Substance?

What is his substance is what so many wants to know but the funny thing is he is still trying to figure what is his substance. Good or Bad there is something he has that a lot of people are searching for SUBSTANCE, everybody needs it but is not easily to obtain. The remaining question is who else among him has the substance everyone is seeking. Our father has substance but many chose not to receive and wonder what is wrong with the way they live so he can sum it up by finding his substance and use it to the fullest. So in his situation substance abuse is a good thing

Treating Others

He treat others the way his father would want him to but no that's not enough they try to misuse his kindness and start talking crazy like he is supposed to be fine with that but he is really tired of treating people with the love of Christ and they want to or try to get him HELLBOUND. What's wrong with that? Everything! But all that is going to change so it's going to be alright because the God we serve know his heart and his thoughts before he knew them. So he decided to keep treating them the way he do and pray that God works on their heart however he see fit... AMEN!!!!

<u>LEARNING!</u>

We learn to hate!

We learn to love!

We learn how to communicate with each other

We learn to be helpful to each other!

We learn all these things and more but when do we do all those

things we learn and why do we do what we do?

 because of the ones who taught us or is it what we see going on

that we learn from watching?

<u>You are there</u>

You are there at his house like a wolf dressed in sheep clothing

Trying to tempt him in ways only the devil himself would do

So if he have to love the hell out of you to make you leave that's

 Exactly what he would do so please don't be disappointed because

 Your expectations in your personal arena of your life didn't play

out like you planned them to be performed

Reality hits hard again

Reality hits hard AGAIN as he rides, walk, and talk to different people in secret in search of the one that make him drop everything he might be doing when she call and be there just for her knowing time will make room for the both of them!

To have or not to have!

Having everything he wanted was a breeze to him because he love to work for his gains but when it came down to finding that special someone he was straight hard headed and a stubborn person who wanted what and who he had love for not settling for anything less but whoever she may be she was second because he wanted so badly to get business established like it should then get on with that part of life. So when the skies around him are clearer in all areas then the questions he seeks after will be answered!

Another Day Another defeat

Once again God reminds him how special and mighty he is in his kingdom by not allowing his mind to take words on paper that man wrote but the words on paper God wrote

Another Day Another Defeat so that will be a yes he is still more than a conqueror. From strength to strength from glory to glory knowing for himself the faith he has will not fail him because it was faith that brought him this far and it will continue to bring him further at a greater measure that he can't even imagine!!!

Yes and maybe yes

Yes he should marry her never mind if she kisses someone else every day! Why she just can't cheat? If he were to care for her it would be too soon and God doesn't move on soon events but timed events with much patience so how can he say he loves her when she tells another man that every day! He truly feels that another time would be the time for them he would do all he knew how to do until then he will continue to push her away waiting on her to figure it out. No many how many visions she might had have regarding the two of them being together because the devil himself could make anything look good to keep or to position us right where he wants us all for the wrong reasons

Not made to be handled

Whatever he were to do he wasn't made to be handled by any human, but God alone so yet they try to place him in certain spots thinking he would give into the area in his life they were trying to handled but did he surprise them. Instead of giving in he became bolder, and wiser. Now he don't care to much for anybody who tries to handle him that way he politely tell them off every time therefore the ones who keep trying to handle him ends up losing his number little do they know he don't care and so what if they find out that only push himself into putting more energy into not caring.

It's The Way

It's the way she walk

It's the way her eyes glisten as he

look into them

It's the way she talk

It's the way she acts

It's the way she thinks

It's the way she look

But bump all that at the end it's the way that he chose

to fall in love with her and only her!!

Waking up every morning

Waking up every morning with her on his mind is the best thing he could ask for but that just at he never ask to be awaken up with her on his mind it's the way God bless him to see another day. As he continues to lay there in his bed and think of other great things they could do besides what every rapper sings about. To him if he were to get paid just to talk about her he would be rich because it wasn't a day that went by that he didn't wake up thinking about her. Not to mention all folks he normally talk to them about her. Nice as it seems he should have known better

Just hanging out

Just hanging out in the late night just the two of them having fun and enjoying each other company giving her every compliment she deserve from head to toe making sure she know he doesn't missed a detail ensuring him that he is letting her know she is greatly appreciated. Especially when it came down to staring or glancing at her pretty face all he could do is think how good he has it to have a friend that looks the way she did with him reminding himself the way she silently stands beside him dishing out great advice when asked helping out when she not asked so he just can't help himself not to fall in love. After all he is just hanging out ....

Changing everything

He changed everything they had planned because more details were now more than ever were clearer because of the motives that would not go or agree with him so he pulled back and went in another direction but in actuality it wasn't him that pulled him in that direction it was God that changed his direction because he had no idea it would go the way it did but it did he just went on the flow of things as they changed so what else could he do? Nothing! but go with the flow that it was going in so what if the ones around him didn't understand because it were the ones that help him go with the flow of things ended up being the ones around him. *Psalm 119:133 King James Version- Order My steps in your word: and let not any iniquity have dominion over me.*

Just The other Day

Just the other day he had started to give up, then he heard how to use a key to open a door he was trying to open for years and it blessed his socks off because it made more sense than ever. He heard it plain and simple the words "If you tell me something maybe I will tell you something" and all this time he thought that was a stage of being shy. So every day he tries his best to tell her something new that she has been known that could make a huge difference in their life in this point of their relationship.

Keep talking please

Keep talking please don't let me stop you from calling him weird because you are not included in his decisions he is making every day for himself. Knowing the only reason why it is like the way it is because it's the mind that we all have that is made different from each other and once you think you have him figured out everything changes putting you back at square one, the square you first met him in not knowing nothing about him at all therefore if God intended for you to be included he will let you know so stop bugging the ones you think could give you answers because they don't even know themselves................ So please keep

TALKING

His Worrying

His worrying wasn't an issue anymore because he laid aside the things that would worry him and picked up the things that worry his one and only true friend as he picks his mind thinking of ways his life could be better for her life to be better which is to him the Godly thing to do which in society you don't hear too much about. But what he thought he would never do is end up……….

But he did. So every morning when he wakes up he does some inner thinking and tells him "today I am going to work for her it is not about me for she will not be stressed out on my behalf she is way to pretty and fragile to be weighed down in such a manner. Trying his best to make that happen he does end up failing a lot of times but the blessed part about the way he thinks is she doesn't even know which is the cool part because doing for others is a ministry of Christ himself and it's okay to him if she never knew that but if she did he would continue in the same pursuit and maybe at a different pace

What does it mean?

What does it mean for a person like that to stay on someone else mind. Trying to shake it off by hanging around others the same manner he hang out with her but it doesn't work out and what do you know he ends back up with her not even mentioning how many times he has tried to break away from her it never works. That alone then got him to thinking well if he care so much about her, which he showed to some very clearly or since for some odd reason he cannot walk out of her life. This one in particular anybody else he wouldn't even think twice about but her the number of times he thought about not leaving her has tripled times a billion and just one day he would know what does it mean?

Made Up Mind

A made up mind that she did have! But made up on what is what no one knew but herself and from the looks of it she wasn't really sure what she wanted to do. Having people in her life that actually cared for her in a physical form didn't seem to concerned for them but all the concern goes out to the ones who she never might see just messages after messages filling up her head and many more with empty promises verses the ones who can and will give her exactly whatever they promised and more. By him constantly looking for signs he constantly keeps finding out the wrong ones but no more now he has a MADE UP MIND…………

A Fulfilling Prayer

A fulfilling prayer it is he really start to realize that when he pray a prayer to our savior Christ that the prayer might have already been answered but he has to work up to that moment. Therefore a lot of rejection is going to come his way a lot of people that he might actually develop feelings for will leave him. Family will take a vow of silence and envy him behind his back. Friends will look at him strange in his own home and actually form the words in their mind to call him weird. By him hearing that he is left with no choice but to MOVE without them knowing anything or hearing any plans about his next big move because sure enough that will give them something to keep talking about. So yes he is enjoying this turbulent times knowing and believing that God will fulfill his prayer and already has just waiting on him to take his position to receive what he have prayed for sop whether it be two steps he need to take to place himself into position or travel to two countries he will do it!..

Clever, Smart, Witty, and Whatever

Yes clever, smart, witty, and whatever were and still is some of the words you can describe the ways of a particular and peculiar individual because he always had this unique way of getting exactly what he wanted and no one really knew how but the man above, Jesus and if you ever ask him he would tell you this "I don't even know myself things in my life have a way of working out for my Good" which many can respect that answer and some can't. The ones that can't accept that is because it's not the answer they were looking for and the ones that do know honest truth once spoken.

A Point

He was at a point of no return he tried to hold on to the words they spoke out of their mouth on several occasions but it proved over and over to be pointless as he searches for one. Just One! And he finds none a disappointment to him indeed because he was in need not in need like a baby but in need of them to honor their word without reminders assuring him they mean what they say, even though he gives them the difference of what they don't do and as he look back trying to make some sense of it all and didn't see no appreciation then and none at this present time either! Therefore to avoid the disappointment he made a point and stopped coming around

Back In Church

Days and months has gone by and the church is still in him but the last he visited and actually fellowship is way off track and is so apparent because he don't even know what's going on right in front of him but yet continue to miss what God has in store for him because he is not in position to receive or is he? Only God knows that but all he know is he needs to straighten up and get back living more of a chased life. Even though many has come and kept going that was trying his belief and his faith and they failed and because they failed their friendship soon followed and faded away also. No regrets on that one just glad to see he can't be bought

Breaking Up

As exciting as his life is more excitement just keeps finding him, yet he is challenged to break up with someone he is not sure they are going together. He tried the tactic that involves bringing others around to see how she would react and the reaction was speechless she didn't show no madness, no anger what so ever! So now he is stuck wondering every night what is going on? Why does he do so much for her but no one does nothing for him? What does it mean? Is his time running out for him or should he keep going to go and test his faith and step out of his made up comfort zone to look for that one who get out the bed for him just to ride to the store.............

Fake Love or Real Love

Up to this point in time he struggles on which fact to zero in on, the fact that its real love or the fact its fake love by him going out the way for a woman that benefits him none that he can see through praying that it is somehow beneficial to the God he serve because if it is fake why must he go all the way out his way to bring peace to her weary soul with the light that is in him even though the life he lives is not a perfect one but to him her life is far more important than his own, seeking everyday he is blessed to live a reason behind all of this……..

Why Stopping

Why stopping is harder than starting he never knew when he would stop the thing he don't want to do but he does it anyway why? He can't even say he just knows of course it's wrong and is getting pretty old! So what ritual or prayer must be embark on? What knowledge must he possess to rid his mind of this activity that keeps playing like a broken eight track in his mind knowing the only thing people don't know is how his past events he was involved in some days beats him up in his mind, he wanting to escape the memories of the past but they keep coming up like spam on an email account.

SWAP!!!!!

If it were possible he would swap but how much he would swap with another how much of his life he would be willing to swap with no regrets leaving all or keeping some why would he keep what he chose to keep and leave what he chose to leave……

The Way

The way she fixes her little eyes on him is a look only she could explain,

a look to him that makes her look so irresistible as if she was trying to convince him to

just run to her fast as he can to embrace her and never let go

and whatever happens after that...

Grown Woman

Grown Woman! Grown Woman! Pick yourself up you don't

have to stay down that is your decision

Grown Woman! Grown Woman! Every relationships has its ups

and downs

But have you tried JESUS?

Grown Woman! Grown Woman! Take back every good thing and

make it better

Of that which people spoke of you will never have again!

Grown Woman! Grown Woman! Christ has given you a new

identity leave

That old identity once and for all and accept your new one I tell

you!

ACCEPT!

This Have To Be Love

The way she makes him feel is a feeling he can't let go of thinking

if only he could spend all day, all night, all week, all month, all

year with her by his side just the two of them he actually might

find himself...... in a place he thought only exist in heaven a place

where the love doesn't grows weaker but stronger and stronger

while he looks back on the days and times he almost gave up on

her and Thank God every morning for keeping him near and the

girl he thought he would and could never find and the girl he

thought he would and could never lose but eventually he did. The

thought that over rides the thought always leaves him asking

himself tons of questions no one he knew could possibly answer

GROWN MAN

Grown Man! Grown Man! Why do you cry all night worrying about your past Dwelling on it will not make the present any better

Grown Man! Grown Man! Get up and be and do what God has Called You to be not man

Grown Man! Grown Man! Prayer is the key not the man next door advice that's

Not even reading the word of God or living a Christ like lifestyle.

Grown Man! Grown Man! GOD has called you and place you into his Kingdom ACCEPT IT!

Kicking Up The Rocks

Kicking up the rocks only to find out you isn't hurting no one but yourself putting all your energy into doing things that really benefit you none it all but for some reason you are comfortable with the things you do creating more tension with damaging your relationship like making a hole in your favorite blanket bigger instead of going to a Fabric Warehouse to purchase a patch kit with a no return policy but it is the life you chose to live because you want to do your own thing so be it!

Forgiveness

The most powerful thing he could do in that week was forgive a friend who completely turned their back soon as he hit a rough area in his life not even a clue why. He once ask himself, "Will I ever speak to her again and on what terms?" he would not ever speak to that friend again and one day he awakes out of his sleep and to his surprise she calls and his first response was in his mind forgive leave the past where it is behind you. Something he has seen many can't do but he carried it out anyway without any hesitation he did exactly that believing that the reason he was contacted is far more important than the reason he might have come up with not to respond back to her in the present.

Why am I here

Is the question he asked over and over as he sat around all those
who said they would be there but no apologizing on their part they
carried on like it never happened or they never said those words
but living in the kingdom of God we pray for a better mind where
does forgetting about the ones who really needs our words given to
us by Christ himself, but as time passed he realized why he was
there? He was there not for people but to hear from the lord!

Confused

Some days she speaks.

Some days she remain silent never telling why but always keeping

him up

All night trying to figure it out why all on his own

Mood swing changes not just because she is a female but from the

events of the day

So once he sees that his mood changes only because he spend too

much time again trying to figure it out not even being sure that

this what he want to tolerate for the rest of his life but for some

reason or another he refuses to leave her. Ignoring the advice from

family and friends saying she don't really know what she want so

he should leave her! Sacrificed things that only God knows about

just for her and he might say once asked why? "I treat everybody

like that ", he is lying only to keep the truth hidden until he feel

what will be a good time and tell her as if she already don't have

enough clues so therefore up until now confused is not even close

to describing his involvements with her……

Body, Soul and Mind

He loves not only the flesh the world sees but everything else the world tries to figure out and still can't see the soul, and the mind all three with one love so strong if he stopped loving the way he did he would develop love withdrawal symptoms causing him to stay up all night singing his own tune of the blues. His favorite is titled "where did I go wrong from loving you" a song that truly represents the body, soul and mind once heard for yourself you might call it a soul cry

<u>YOU!</u>

You filled his head up with hopes and dreams reasons for him to

hold his head up high to slow down his suffering brought on by

others he surrounded himself with but instead you did the

opposite adding on to the list of worries he never paid any

attention to by leading him on with a bunch of false and empty

promises and hopes more reasons more to hold his head down if

he chose to rejoicing in the fact that JESUS is not like that, so he is

left with no regrets but to cut you off all the ways you thought he

was attached to you. So while you would rather do he would

rather not so put those two words together and don't bother trying

to find a way that acceptable by him to say you are sorry

A Good Break Indeed

All this time he was wondering why out of the blue their friendship ended. He prayed about it and everything! All he did is give out advice and teach through his experiences about life and what to expect out of it when becoming of that age when asked or not what he thought the things he was hearing and being discussed at the time. He didn't get mad in fact he just realize it was a good deed indeed she executed out because if he was always there for her how would she learn the point he was making ? Therefore he was glad the day that the friendship started back up to see the things he were telling then is still being applied and she really didn't ignore him back then nor today…..Now he just ask himself questions targeted towards his Father a reason why they split up the way they did? Why did he allow them to reunite the way he did? Is there something else he has in store for them? When will he revealed them? But of course man will try to steer him and in all different directions but all he is going to do is pray and believe!

He See….

He see little bits of images in his mind that he eventually make it to pictures in his mind turning those pictures in his mind into movies in his mind of the greater things and events to come and to all little bits of pieces of doing wrongful things they stay as he first see them incomplete. Being who he is and from listening to a lot of others thoughts and being asked for input all the time he struggles daily to keep his mind free and clear and isn't afraid to tell anyone that because he believes firmly that to live for you and not everybody else is a fight we must fight daily!

Caught Up in a Fantasy

Living life the way she thought she could only in a fantasy ignoring the real facts she is faced with outside her fantasy avoiding the one who truly loves her with few words and actions only in a fantasy world that exists only in her mind preventing herself from moving forward in life itself because of the amount of time she has dedicated to this fantasy world of hers making it more difficult every day to the one that loves her unconditionally that took quite some time for him to do knowing she has been in this fantasy world is no match for the real world the exact reason why she never let her two worlds collide assuming that if they do she would be left in that fantasy world without too much concern from the real world including him, a fantasy that should have ended a long time ago like a tree that has stop bearing fruit it eventually die from lack of attention therefore she gets what she pay for but everything that looks good isn't.

<u>AFRAID!!!!!</u>

Afraid to love him but you quote "Love me like you want to be love", but once he does that he gets no attention I mean a little affection will not hurt but so afraid to love he never knowing why he just know he is getting tired of pouring out his love. How long will this carry on or is this just an illusion of the heart or is she that hurt on the inside from past relationship she ignores true love starring her right in the face. The saddest part of it all is that everyone sees how much he loves her but her

Torture

The only thing that's on his temporary list but he tries to make it permanent. All night and during the day you will find him talking about this one particular girl ignoring the word of God he strongly use to believe in settling for this girl that has his mind so gone he do anything she ask him to do ignoring the consequences if any that follow his actions she never knowing all this keeps him in a torture stage wanting to be set free from all of it but he hesitates on doing just that which only requires him to open up his mouth and just tell her how he really feels but by him trying to predict every move he don't tell her because it might damper their relationship but now it's getting real stressful on him because he wants to move forward with him or not but whatever choice be made is fine with him because he is a gentleman who really cares in a way that he is fine with her decision knowing what the God he served has promised him prevents him from breaking out in anger something he has been deliver from for quite some time or from feeling hurt, after all it is what it is feelings making vows and promises to himself he would not go into another year feeling tortured in his own mind when he has complete control over the situation.

The Definition of Feelings

Something that never stays the same in no situation each day a
new feel arrives to the mind that's in the brain connected to the
central nervous system that then send electrical impulses up and
down the nervous system including the spinal cords located in the
back so therefore he cannot feel the way he was yesterday due to
the fact that a new day has arrive with new information that the
mind takes in and process it whether it's good or bad based on the
way he feel from that his actions are made clear to many and
misunderstood to many

Ruining

Yep ruining his life with this relationship that isn't going nowhere despite all the things he has been doing all he ever gets is a thank you but maybe one day he will have a home cooked meal or something different that says "You Mean the World To Me". Not even once but since this year is about over a new dawn is approaching he now tries figuring out what needs to be left with the year he no longer lives in and what needs to be brought over into this glorious year he approaches boldly, and one thing for certain he would no longer be ignoring the word or the voice of the Lord to please a girl that appears to be not trying to hear what he might have to say or a word that would save her soul from damnation WORD OF GOD! Ruin but yet salvageable to be made new again.

Loving

Loving is what it became once he started putting God first in all things. He no longer wondered is she the one. He knows sees that she is the one. Support when you need it, comfort when you least expected it! All of his and more continue to surprise him every day they see each other. Reminding her that she is real close to fulfilling certain scriptures and is setting her up for a much bigger blessing a blessing that will overtake her. The things they both use to stress or worry about will soon be a thing of the pass and only one man to thank his name.

The Road

They are on a road, a positive road of uncertainly not knowing where this road is going to take them they both take it not rushing on this road but taking time to learn the things needed to know while on this road with patience they both know only time will tell them their true purpose on this road they chose to travel together with no regrets interesting as they both are willing to travel to the end.

Him meeting Her

Him meeting her had to be ordained by God; why else would he reach out to a complete stranger? She speaks words of a wise woman but yet young, a level of maturity many are still trying to reach but she has reached it and excel in them not straying away from what she has been taught but embraced it to a point that attracts or hook up with like spirits

Living this new life

Living this new life as a new creation hasn't been this easy until he gave it all up to God.

The vehicles he use to drive to his sin he didn't want to let go until he got tired of not

Fulfilling the life God had planned for him that one last time. Which was to him a sure indication that the lifestyle he was living not to many knew or even showed some concerned about whatever he was doing therefore he thought might as well keep living doing the same old thing, until he got the true revelation of seeking GOD first in all things he was a part of.

Psalm 53:2 King James Version-God looked down from heaven on the children of men, To see if there were any that did understand, that did seek God.

Mistreated Only for a While

Sometimes being mistreated first is the first step to actually walking into your destiny with the right one who will never mistreat you which is Christ. Then the person who is operating in the spirit of Christ then your fulfillment in him will not be far away. Knowing when we exercise our faith in any and all things our tears will turn into tears of joy which could be the very next minute!!!

Psalm 126:5 They that sow in tears shall reap in joy. KJV

A Renewed Love

A renewal takes place in his mind rebuilding the love he thought he lost with his father first as he continue to do that he is shown clearly where his support would come down in at looking back on the day he was thirsty and now he thirst no more knowing if he actually needed a drink of water in this world he would get a case.

Away He went

Away he went into the hills on the road with destiny in his heart with one purpose in mind. A way to come back better than the way he left not just for him but for others God speaks to him about. Others he thought wouldn't mind being brought out of their environment believing in the fact that the atmosphere plays a major role in one's destiny with Christ.

Away he went not looking for handouts but looking for the things that were promised to him by his father.
away he went desperately seeking a change this very second with no second
thoughts of how things will pan out once he get to his new destination. All he knew is Change is got to come.

Highly Favored

Highly favored was he indeed. Impacting lives everywhere he went without even knowing the words to speak until the very last second. Never doubting the gospel he always had a word that connects with their inner man.

Seeing that he was highly favored he figures he might as well minister until God himself

Speaks to him and say REST MY GOOD AND FAITHFUL SERVANT, REST

Calling All Unbelievers

Hear Ye! Hear Ye! Calling all unbelievers a time is coming upon you and the rest of them that continue to operate in such a manner! REPENTANCE needs to come to your idle ways of thinking. Our father is not pleased at how you yet continue to try to hinder what and who he has called blessed! How dare you to try to even speak in that manner and you know he says Touch ye not my anointed nor do my prophets any harm, but don't listen to the warning you just been given and wait and see what happens next......

1 Chronicles 16:22 King James Version- Saying, Touch not mine anointed, and do my prophets no harm.

Getting Weary

Lord send your angels to comfort him, he is feeling weak from enduring the tests and trails that comes his way knowing they only last a moment and when they are all over he will continue to give you all the glory, all the honor, and all the praise

Given the Words

Given the words to bring the lost to a better understanding of Christ and the ways of Christ is what he enjoyed doing the most. To him that was his nine to five.

Given the words knowing what not to speak beforehand but he knew if God sent them to him he had a word for them. A reason why through his obedience his cup continues to overflow

God give him strength

God give him strength to help the ones you would have him to help

God give him strength to look beyond his circumstances to give

others the spirit of you that dwells in him, the Holy Ghost

God give him strength to endure these rough times he is faced with

God give him strength to continue to minister your word unto all

you put in his path with no hindrances

God give him strength…..

GOD GIVE HIM STRENGTH…..

How many times

How many times must he start over?

How many times must he lose to gain?

How many times must he be heartbroken before he meets up with

a True love that never departs?

How many times he has to leave those wolves dressed in sheep

clothing

Oh Lord guide him through these times he is to a point in life

that's requiring divine intervention

Free but yet still bound

Free from the white walls physically but yet emotionally bound by his surroundings' feeling like a stage of entrapment he desperately want to escape from so he can be free totally from the snares of this world so then he would surely be FREE TO WORSHIP, but until then he presses on fighting the good fight of Faith knowing it's just a matter of time God will deliver him from the hands of the enemy!

Facial Expressions

The face you made at the playground on one particular day in his mind at that moment he could only think "she is still cute and more adorable when she does that" but little does she know ....His love for her just grows stronger each time he is around her no matter how many times he tries to deny that he is not in love with her his when asked about her his conversation says otherwise. Going the distance enjoying their time they can spend with each other until things become more permanent and that rock like no other goes on her finger. But how long does this feeling should last is the question all can wonder. Will they ever make it together to the paradise he has created in his mind?

Finally Revealed

A time is upon him to reveal the way he really feel about her, resisting his feelings and not telling her has never helped. He has to get over some type of fear that he might have that prevents him from telling how he have been feeling for years. Running from telling her always have him regretting he ran. Now since he knows the truth he prays that in God's due time he will do the separation needed to be done because if it were left up to him he wouldn't do it. Knowing that it wasn't going to be that easy for him to do what needed to be done since the years he feel kind of in a cycle but don't know how he got so sidetrack or if he is on track in that cycle. He knew what to look for and fell for at the same time. A true eye opener for him actually knows now how spirits disguise themselves that only brings him to wonder more!

Forgiveness Does Come

Forgiveness does come, to the ones that are receiving what God has planned for them, and to the ones that don't know the plan God has for them. But to be able just to say forgive me if he caused any harm or misunderstandings and the response he gets is you haven't done anything wrong but the only thing wrong with this is never tell anyone that you haven't done anything wrong if he ask for forgiveness because you never knew the secret thoughts that goes through his mind that he was actually freeing his self from so he can stop holding up what God has in store for him. So yes forgiveness does come from God and from Him…...

He Caught A Glimpse

He had caught a glimpse of a lifestyle he would leave everything behind, a glimpse of one of his Fathers promises and enjoyed every bit of it until it came to an end leaving him questioning himself. To him there was no reason to end. A little suffering wouldn't hurt especially if his father suffered why not them, why not him. But no it's not a them anymore it's just him but as God mends his heart he learns the True meaning of love, The real Ministry of The Saints

Led by God or man

Being led by God in all his situations didn't and wasn't an easy choice but being led by strange men and women would of course be easy another trick of the enemy No Doubt But due to his relationship with his father his discernment is kicked up another notch as he realized endurance is the key in all situations never straying away from the truth just the lies they keep up not knowing he is casting then down at the same time. What are the chances of them figuring that out.........

MAD AS HELL!!!

What's wrong with him? He is mad as hell at the enemy the devil himself draining the children of Christ with all this nonsense slipping spirits in which the children of Christ is doing their best to make it above the rest, so the enemy keeps placing people around surroundings they need not to be in but until that day of deliverance comes they must fight the good fight of faith, Mad as Hell because what's going on with the children of Christ so yes he is taking it to a personal level and will be praying and casting down certain spirits that rises up against him because he is free from the weighs of this world he don't care who he leave or who support him knowing that this time will pass our God we serve will not bring us this far to leave us. Mad as Hell but he is about to call down Heaven.................!!!!

<u>MISSED ONE</u>

Missed one is the number he missed the most. They spoke truth and didn't mind telling like it is once lead to speak on the matter at the time. Which now is missed the most needing that second opinion on some life changing decisions but the foremost first major change out of all is to become one, so there want be no missed one. Just one as they unite together doing the kingdom exploits God has placed inside both of them to do.

My House

My House was a real ran down one. Windows busted anything could have come in, not to mention if they are trying to get warm they could hang that up. Doors off the hinges anything could have walked or crawl in but the floor boards were also rotten. So all quests invited and uninvited would fall in therefore giving thieves and liars an open invitation and the foundation my house was built on started to crumble. But soon as he found the solid rock he started to build again but this time on a solid foundation which is Christ himself the hope of Glory. So that means nobody isn't just walking in no more without an invite from the father himself so if you get turned away at the door, it's nothing personal................

Haggai 1-King James Version

No one to call

No one to call to tell them they will be missed, no one to call while he is away from his hometown. He can't help but to wonder why should he go back, He is not going to lie if given the opportunity he would most definitely make a new happy home in uncharted territory for him. Who really knows what and how his father is planning for his life. No one but a prophet that can be a drunk off the streets……..or an animal.

Pleasant

Oh how pleasant is she walking strong in her faith determined to make a change in her life knowing that God has a plan for her life not settling for the things of this world but shunning away from them with all her heart. Not looking down on one thing of the world and looking up to the other thing in the world. Being thirsty for only one thing and one thing only water that represents the spirit of Christ Himself not being easily moved but holding firm to her faith that God has the best and he is the best. There is NOBODY GREATER! Searching diligently for just someone to love her for her as Christ does nothing more or nothing less realizing that real love will never leave her side no matter what she is going through just as Christ has never left her side either OH! How pleasant it is.........

Revived

Here he sits feeling abused, hurt, misused to a certain extent but that doesn't break him it builds him up knowing that God has raised up a standard. Then one day God had placed in his heart to visit this place we have visited before. As he was desperately seeking for answers and had some questions. As he proceeds of course the enemy was whispering in his ear you late don't go, but that night he heard the voice of God say go anyway. And as he went to that particular place God met him there hearing a confirming word and before he left the prophet spoke. Now more than ever he is doing the will of God and whatever comes along to throw him off from his revived state he make another road believing what the prophets spoken therefore he must do what he got to do regardless of who don't like it.

The Call

The call which some ignore he fully accept. There is nothing else in the world to actually do; he has tried it his way it didn't work. The world has tried to recruit him and it still didn't work. The funny part is they put so much hope in him to do what they wanted him to do he ran without looking back because that's not what God has called him to do. Knowing they are far from understanding the way he see so the best thing he do is depart.

There when Needed

Please don't tell him you are him for him just because the words he is speaking at the moment for once you have been there but what about the times when he didn't need you, will you still be here just out of love and admiration, to hold, to cherish, to wake you up in the morning to tell you about a vision God gave him while he was sleep. There when needed only time will tell but he doesn't need just words followed by no action he needs comfort, support, affection...........and so much more!

This is the time

This is the time to operate in faith harder than ever before.

The time to say what needs to be said.

The time to do what needs to be done for the righteous

must take a stand these are times we are living in!

Year by Year we are being too passive and not active

Through it all what he thought it was it was the complete opposite

but going through it only made him strong. Being a fact that if he

go through it by himself never to look back upon that moment

moving forward and God ward so his will get done giving God all

the praise

BE FREE OR BE BOUND...........

When everything else has failed

When everything else has failed, what then he do? He did the only thing God didn't script away from him which was his gift from the beginning but due to so many influences that look good at the time like the cars, the money, and pretty much anything else that wasn't of Christ but spoke to be at that time went.. So it was a Job like experience only from him and due to the calling upon his life which he understands

Fight

Don't mess with me, this is not what you want to do.

This fight you are not going to win. I boldly proclaim that before you start this fight.

The reason why is because of my father that dwells in me who is with me, my habitation, my refugee, my rock. So if you still want to fight

I am going to tell you this one last thing I haven't met or heard of anyone that has won a fight with my father nope not one.........

If he told you

If he told you how much he really cared

for you would you believe him

If he told you he tried putting you out his mind leaving you as a

thing of the past but you always come back up to his present day

giving him great futuristic views but see that just how the enemy

dress it up sometimes to keep you in a place that will distract you

from what God is telling him to do, so much that it almost becomes

a soul tie

If he told you what and how much you mean to him what would be

your response? How would you react? See that just the case if he

don't stay lost in the word the devil has a way of making him lost

on an issue that he makes up in his mind.

If he told you that there is not a day that goes by without him

thinking about you, and how glad he is in this present day to longer feel the agony, hurt, or pain you knew or didn't knew you put him through. Now that's freedom

To care for you in so many ways praying to God to not let you take priority over his praise, worship, and prayer life with his father but after all was said and done it brought him closer to all those. This shows him that God has a unique way about perfecting his word that he has put in him that no man can take out

Remembering the time

Remembering the moment they shared for the first time. A moment of intimacy hugged up all night. He never knew what she was thinking but in his mind there ran so many questions. So many thoughts, heart pumping really fast then it slowed down to the normal. And when it was all over. That moment was never spoke of again but the thought of it is relived in his mind everyday wishing that moment could have lasted for ever but as time went on God delivered him from that thought because it was not of him. But it became another blockage in his mind that prevented him from hearing the word the way God was speaking to him. Therefore it only proves that the devil himself can create Good moments that cater to his flesh but yet the secret motive it to hold him back from his Father but one thing the devil knew and was reminded of is that God is Not Mock……..

Galatians 6:7 King James Version- Be not deceived, God is not mocked: for whatsoever a man soweth, that shall he also reap

Accident on Standby

There he goes into his stages of worrying. An accident waiting to happen but is at an accident of sorrow? An accident of actually falling in love? Holding it all together wanting to desperately to just be able to walk up to her and ask her " how can a person hang around another person for years and not think about being with the person they are around" Yes is the answer he received after he thought of that statement . But the amazing part about this accident on standby really isn't an accident. He has to wait because real love is not obtained by being anxious but with patience.

An accident on standby with no planned location.

No planned time it could happen anywhere they happen to be or anywhere God sends him in a different direction.

Words

Certain words he thought he could never tell anyone again not even to his family because of the past relationships with certain family and friends. Words that meant or carried a lot of weight once said just not by him but you out of all people he knew professionally, personally, and in church. You brought it out of him without sweating to do it. Unknowingly he had trouble because she never told you yet so as the moon changes so does him. So there will be more words than ever spoken of the truth this year he knew for a fact he wouldn't say again but love will bring light to anything thought of to be put to rest.

Waiting to Unveil

It's not that he thinks about you every day and night it's just not

the time nor the place but God allows and grants us the time

but it's in His time that it became the right time and the right

place.

Then he can tell you what he have been wanting to tell you the first

time he look into your eyes

Punk out Spirit

His life surely has gotten harder but one thing he won't do is punk
out.

There have been ones that comes into his life and left a month
later.

Punk out because their mind couldn't handle the move of God

upon his life, because they didn't have enough faith n their own

situations so why did he expect them to have faith on his situation

making him more stronger than ever for being

what God called him to be and leaving those fools as God would

call them, but there is yet still hope

Through it all

Through all the hell he has been through and all the heaven that was revealed to him. Only one remained that I can truly love. Leaving the past where it is at, in the sea. Not constantly reminding me of things in the past but helping achieve the goals of this present day. It's like an angel keeps whispering in his ear. Do it! Go for it! You want fail you have my support! It will work out be patient even though that one don't understand everything, don't let that stop them from supporting what's your everything. That's Real Love Through It All

Thanking God

Thanking God the way he eased my trouble mind giving him strength to continue to run this race he has me in to win. Knowing he is more than a conqueror, remaining victorious in every battle he is faced with not looking back to how it could have been but looking up and moving forward in a God-ward way. Believing him for those things to come as he said in his word "Believe the prophets and so shall you prosper" never doubting or complaining but with oil of gladness he will continue to have praise on his heart and will never stop praying for the known and the unknown. Therefore knowing what God has in store for him it is for him. Which no man can give or take.

2 Chronicles 20:20 King James Version- And they rose early in the morning, and went forth into the wilderness of Tekoa: and as they went forth, Jehoshaphat stood and said, Hear me, O Judah, and ye inhabitants of Jerusalem: Believe in the Lord your God, so shall ye be established; believe his prophets, so shall ye prosper.

If you were happy for him

You know a friend you were called to him but your title fit the way you treated him. A question you can only answer. Beating yourself up trying to compute all these things and more. But if you were happy for him your whole persona would have not changed. If you would have remembered how wise he was... would you still have befriended him? But that's where the wolf actually get exposed and is no longer hidden dressed in sheep clothing because if you were able to turn on him with a quicken spirit like you knew all along. Which you did knew your time was going to be up he was never obligated to be there for you but he tried but time and time again little appreciation was shown. So what was shown is all he needed to see which was so clearly. So find it not strange if you do feel strange because he is in a much happier place with his body, mind, and soul and there is absolutely nothing you could say or do to change that. So continue to lie to yourself and call him friend but friends don't continue to misuse and mislead each other.

Thank You Lord

Thank You Lord for revealing to him the thing that held him back and down instead of up and forward. For years have went by and he became passive to people running in and out of his life hurting as they please to, but he thinking not to argue with him or confront them but to say to himself he don't bother him. That only meant he was lying and to himself and to the Holy Spirit. Even though God knew he wanted him to release it but year after year he held it in up until now he has the revelation when the word of God stated to cast every weigh he only cast some. Thinking since he told certain individuals that he forgives them for hurting him. But he didn't give it to God and the devil knew that the area he wouldn't give up would be the area God wants to bless him in but he is no more blind to that fact due to the help of the Ministry of The Saints he has gain a much clearer understanding of how holding all that in and not giving it all up to God can and will turn into pride. But since he now knows the truth he his making his

REQUESTS KNOWN!!!

Philippians 4:6 KJV Be careful for nothing; but in everything by prayer and supplication with thanksgiving let your requests be made known to God.

His Handy Helper

Truly handy is not the proper word to use but its catchy because the things she has taught him throughout the years about dedication, support, patience, virtue, encouragement.......and so much more is more than handy. If he had to put a price on how handy she is heaven will go bankrupt being more valuable than the finest rubies, diamonds, and pearls. The way she has been there through the years just bring tears sometimes when God awakens him up to reflect on things to better plan his next move. Never once thought he will find a friend like this but in the midst of their storms they found each other. Never arguing with her on anything but coming to an agreement even though that's all his family seems to do, doesn't mean he has to and if anybody ever ask who keeps motivating him besides God to keep going in the direction he is going in he tells them "a very special friend of mine" leaving her name out of the conversation but not out of his mind in the event that his two feet should walk away from her it won't be long before they run back being that he is not stupid and recognize that he is not settling for less because to him she is the best in spite of what the hell everyone else thinks however his handy helper is more than just Handy helper

The Perfect Christmas Gift

This Christmas what he has always wanted and got this year. Which is someone he can share his dreams with, text two in the morning if he can't go to sleep, share with her what he use to fear but not no more, missing her presence the second she is out of his sight. Creating memories that last a lifetime, what more could he ask for when he already has

THE PERFECT CHRISTMAS GIFT!!!!

Beauty Defined

Well he is left in amazement again as she walks away only for a while, and the only word that comes to mind is just GORGEOUS-Beauty Defined. Not just off the way she looks but by the way she carries herself, and her way of thinking is way off any chart he has seen or read. Trying his best not to let her know that the best part of his days that can get better is with her. So whoever said it's impossible to define beauty was just an opinion because he has defined it, which is all of her. A beauty many search for their whole lifetime but he doesn't have to search a whole lifetime for. He can move forward now to greater things in life. Oh what Beauty, a Beauty that can't be framed but only held in his arms for eternity.

Overwhelmed On Every Side

Everything he did he did to his best, loving ones that he wasn't even quite sure loved him back. Doing the most for everybody and doing the less for himself which puts what he needed to do last at the end of the day, when he tired and overwhelmed surely by that time he don't even have the strength. The saddest part of it all is doing what he is doing he surly cannot hear from God the way he need to. Realizing that he is constantly looking desperately for a way out wanting to just throw all up in the air and walk the other way without looking back. Part of him feel like just leaving it all behind. The friend he grew to love so much, the school he is attending, the current Job occupations he currently holds on to with all his might the family, the friends; then there is a part of him that want to stay. He is so far gone he don't know what to really do anymore, how to properly respond to certain situations in his life that need to be dealt with without prolonging any more time. This feeling will come to an end, those two different feelings he has will come to one ultimate decision and right about now that's not a bad idea. Knowing he should pray for those who continually to spitefully use him but it just gets to a point where he is at in life he feels like he cannot take no more praying that God give him a resolution out of his Love, Not out of His anger because any decision that is made while angry is normally the wrong decision. Overwhelmed only for a short while but God will get the Glory out of this as well............

If I Am....

I f I am hungry she will give me her last

If I am in a storm she will go through it with me

If I am in need she is in need

If I am lost for words she will find them for me

If I am being to forgetful she steps in and pick up the slack

If I am without and she has it I am not without anymore

If I need someone to talk to she makes herself available at any given time

If I wanted to just walk down the street she will walk with me.

If I wanted company to just chill and relax with she is there

If I am down her cheerful spirit pick me up

If I am who God called me to be, then she is who God called her to be

If I am which I was, but now everything I have is hers, and what is hers is mine what a beautiful union.

Only One

If he had only one true friend instead of twenty fake friends he could avoid the confusion, the frustration, the liars, and anything else that is not of God. Knowing liars can't be trusted. So he don't mind at all if that one friend is all he have which will keep him at peace. One friend that keeps it honest in the midst of this perverse society and at the end of the day if the only thing he has to reflect on the times they share and continue to share will be alright with him. One friend that keeps him straight in his personal life and in his business life what else could he ask for in that one friend if she isn't already doing what he has been wanting to ask her. One friend will always be better than those twenty fake ones

The way she thinks

He never knew how she would respond or what she might say that she has been thinking about. But when she do her words skip whatever they have to skip and hit the heart where it matters the most. If her words were a drug he would have been addicted by now but for this addiction no rehab is needed bringing out the better man in him, and killing certain thoughts mentally at the same time. You will think she paid a lot of money to be taught to think that way, but the truth is gifts come without repentance. If he would say so himself her mind is fine-tuned with her heart, one thing for certain he would listen to her all night and if he fall asleep listening he would make up craving more!

If she was a bird

If she was a bird she will be the prettiest and rarest of them all, no need to look no further. A bird that will never see isolation and if she does it will be with him. A bird that sees no limits, and one he would never get tired of seeing, or being around. A bird that will never see any hurt, harm or danger but the total opposite care to the utmost and unconditional compassion that will never die inside of him but grows stronger and stronger each second of the minute, each minute of the hour, day, week, month and years when she is in his presence and out of his presence. The way this bird makes him feel no one can explain that better than him, a feeling he wouldn't trade for nothing in this world she has truly captured his heart!

Just who she is...

Looking gorgeous everyday no matter what she has on, it's not none other out there that carries what she carries, you will never catch him complaining but always appreciating every second of her time, every thought she brings to his attention, all her honesty he can't even think of doing anything wrong to her but everything right and loving to both of their satisfaction. What else to be said? It's just who she is

The Works

The works of God never stop in his life no matter what's going on. He now see that as God begins to transform his surroundings and including the people he hung around. Majority of those people were drop off his list of friends due to the Spirit of Christ that dwell within him, enjoying the new thing God is doing this year in the midst of everything, thankful for being led by the spirit even though Satan tried his best to draw him from among the one (s) that will benefit him the most in the natural and in the spirit. As he pray "Lord let your will be done, continue to transform my surroundings make everything new. I don't care what I leave behind. So I thank you Lord in advance for taking me from glory to glory, thank you in advance for your grace you continue to bestow upon me so that I may continue to Overcome and remain Victorious......AMEN"

Where could they be?

Who would stand in the gap and pray, who would just stand on someone else behalf without throwing it up in their face. Who said He, WHO! How long must we continue to feel like there is not to many standing in the gap as they claim, if they were why hasn't God revealed something to them about the ones they are standing in the gap for which would only confirm what they already knew. So where could they be? Looking in the church and found none, but found something greater outside the church and became a better church all together. That's what happen when they stopped looking and turn it over to the King of Kings!!!

To Be or Not to Be a Fool

To be or not to be a fool is the question he must answer himself at times like this knowing the tactics of the enemy normally and as usual would sneak in through who he thought he LOVED the most but the more he watch. Could it be he was so blinded that he only seen what he wanted to see? Or was it that he knew in his heart something kept him there, as time passed on that something that kept him there in that place was later be known as God.

He Had to Swear

He had to swear to his own hurt

 never to be hurt again

He had to swear to his own abuse

Never to be abused again

He had to swear to his own neglect in the mind

never to be neglected mentally again

He had to swear to the bad relationships that left him feeling in a

stage of depression creating blocks in his mind to never get in

those relationships again but for God to heal or eliminate

whatever caused those things he had to swear by so it will not

hinder the blessing God has in store for him. Knowing if he didn't

those same tactics the enemy used to put him in those situations

would work every time, so he had to swear no other option!

Just Wanting To

He just want to be with her no worldly reason why, he wants to be by her side through it all to help her get to where she is going in life. Oh! Yes he is more than willing, so willing he had thought doing the greatest thing a man can do so many times. Looking for anybody else in her category is pointless because he knows he will find no other greater treasure more valuable than her, she stays in a league that's untouchable not to be mistaken for competition because she doesn't have to compete. The only one that can change that is Christ the Hope of Glory in Her!!!

He Lack No More

There used to be time where he thought his life wasn't moving to the way God had intended it to, overcame some areas of life and still overcoming the others. But one day he met the most joyous beautiful woman, a woman after God's own heart. The way she makes him feel he can't even describe, he just know it's a feeling he don't want to go away. Taking her time to correct him, being strong in the areas he is weak in…it's just so much she do that it leaves him to be the most Grateful person never taking her for granted

His Goodness and Mercy

Lord it is your goodness and mercy that kept him even when he was in iniquity. Lord it's your goodness and mercy lead him to the places he was going not knowing what God had in store for him he just knew he had to go that route. Knowing faith is relying solely upon his father whether he see it or not. But because of his faith he is blessed beyond his comprehension.

Lord it's your Goodness and Mercy brought him to the things he thought once upon a time he never will have.

His Goodness and Mercy continue to shield him no longer being in iniquity but delivered from all that had him shackled, the yokes has been removed, the soul ties has been broken, Liars don't even stay in his presence and if they think he is fooled they got a surprise coming their way in the Name of Jesus

Missing Her The Most

He is at a very challenging point in his life, taking huge risks and doing the craziest things to make better than before even though he admitted to not putting God first which he does now without no procrastination, not to mention his faithful, never doubting, always supportive, encouraging, and uplifting friend that stands with him, talks with him, and walks with him in the storms he is face with. By her being all that and more he miss her the most. A week without her by his side is straight torment to him because when they're together all he see is increase all around. ALL AROUND!!!

God Showed Him

God showed him, himself as he went through what many may called a rough patch in life. But while it was rough God showed him everything about himself to a point where he thought he was different but he was really the same as them due to the fact of them not doing as the Word of God states, and he stops or start being slack in doing what the Word states becoming more like them and less like Christ coming to a conclusion that he had engaged in so much conversation with everyone else but God, that only open up a door and gave the devil place to come on in, which surely prevented him from hearing what God had to say…..so now after God showed Himself he is humble as a dove

Two Broken Hearts Equals One

Two broken hearts equals one whole heart, the heart of God himself. As they continue listening to the voice of God throughout the day. The two find peace and understanding leading them more into their breakthrough. Unsure where God is taking them but more than willing to go, reassuring each other that there will be no more hurt, there will be no more regrets, there will be no more broken hearts, there will be no more sorrow but joy! Unspeakable joy as he is blessed to see the next day realizing the very thing he has needed has been there all along. Allowing God to renew both of their minds giving them more peace of mind to operate fully in his kingdom

<u>It was all too easy</u>

It was all too easy for him to give up what he didn't need for the simple reason they was not beneficial to him at all. So when the one that was a help mate to him was placed in his path by his father he had to accept that the best deserve the best and not nothing less, and that's exactly how she is viewed to him and to anybody else when he asked about her. Now he no longer sit up all night wondering why he keeps getting pimped, draining his anointing. Now he is strengthen knowing he can rejoice in the fact of the things that are added to him through the spirit from her words he gets so lost in reminding him it's the same way he is lost in Christ. And vice versa a prayer he prayed just don't remember when because God has already answered the prayer but he was out of place to receive the answer from the prayer. So you know by now there is not a day that don't go by without him Thanking the Lord for her and everything else.

Letting Go Everyday

Whew! His days are getting more solid knowing that God is doing a great work in the midst of what he might call circumstance. Realizing God is greater than any issue he is facing because all his needs has already been met one reason why he don't worry about nothing. Praying for the things known and unknown knowing it isn't about his time it's all about GOD'S TIME a time no man can beat but many will try and end up in the pit of hell if not stopped sooner. Releasing to God Total control in all areas of his life everyday not just the days he attend Church and by doing just that God is yet constantly pouring down blessings after blessing upon him. Never forgetting the fact you can't beat God giving to his children that He calls Friend. Just doing what he has been doing dedicating his life back to Christ more and more in his everyday walk knowing there will be people who is going to try to get him to break his faith. People on assignment from the devil himself but you better believe he is praying everyday putting up that hedge of protection around him remember hearing the word of his Father *"No weapon Formed Against Me Shall Prosper -Isaiah 5:17 KJV"* and the other scripture " *Touch ye not my anointed nor do my Prophets any harm-1 Chronicles 16:22 NIV"*. HE wasn't joking!!!

The King in Search of a Queen

Living the way God has planned is the best plan ever for him.

Living that type of life but no one around to share it with was not

a great thing for him looking and observing the people inside his

circle wondering to himself could this friend of his be his queen.

The qualities he look for does not all come from curves but brains.

A queen indeed that will help him in this lifestyle he now has not

to hinder. Someone who could be able to give him that comfort of

knowing that the king she is with will not let his queen fall,

hunger, thirst or go in need or want of anything. And if she does it

will be because he is away from her.

Containing The Love

His love was so great only God had actually won all of that. But there have been some who has tried to contain his love but they failed because his love is like a river that never runs out or dry up, it keeps pouring out and sometime more love. That's where he thought the problem was but to his surprise it wasn't him. It was the ones who tried to obtain his love they were nowhere or not even close to being equipped properly also meaning taught on how to handle such love because once his love is obtain it just automatically shifts to greater and greater things in the power of love which comes down from heaven as his father stated "If I lose it Heaven , I will lose it in Earth…"And that's exactly what he did he poured out his love upon him with the love he has already had in his Heart. So a warning is now being issued to the one that actually obtains this love-

THERE IS GOING TO BE A LOVE EXPLOSION!

EXPLOSION!

Added Light

Added light by a source unexpected but greatly appreciated. Kind of snuck up on him at that time. Thinking to himself he must hold on to this added light like a newly discovered treasure he had to tighten his grip. He had to come up with more ways to not let this light pass him again. While holding on to the light at the same time praying to God what must he do on his behalf to keep this great light source? But was he equipped spiritually to harness this light. Thinking that this is the type of light he could use in his breakthrough knowing when two lights combine they just shine brighter blinding everybody who is used to being in darkness not caring who they were in darkness. So his only focus is now this great light source. He refuses to go another day without it! Loving the fact that it becomes a permanent addition for then certain principalities and demonic spirits will be defeated and returned back to the sender.

References Used throughout book

https://biblehub.com

Made in the USA
Monee, IL
19 May 2021

68040566R00095